A Diamond From Clay

Volume One

The Process of the Unseen

Dawn S. Shoats

Copyright © 2026 by Dawn S. Shoats

All rights reserved. No part of this book may be reproduced, distributed, or transmitted in any form or by any means, including photocopying, recording, or other electronic or mechanical methods, without the prior written permission of the publisher, except in the case of brief quotations embodied in critical reviews and certain other noncommercial uses permitted by copyright law.

ISBN: 979-8-9946536-0-9

Published by Diamond Clay Publishing

Dedication

To the little girl in me. I see you. Finally.

Acknowledgments

First and always, I acknowledge God—El Shaddai, The Almighty One, and El Roi, the God who sees me.
You saw me when this work was only a whisper. You carried me when my courage failed. You reminded me that this process was purposeful. This book exists because You sustained me.

To my husband, there are so many things I could say. You've been on this journey with me. You are my protector and my confidant. When I needed reassurance, and presence, you held me. Firmly and gently. You wiped tears and helped me find language when I didn't have words. You covered me in prayer. NO ONE could ever hold this space. It takes a *you*, to love a *me*.

To my children, you challenged me in unimaginable ways. Loving you has shaped me, stretched me, healed me, and taught me more about grace than I ever expected.
To my precious granddaughter, you have a place in my heart. As you grow, I pray that wisdom will be yours and that you let your light shine to glorify God in heaven.

To my grandsons—twins! Double the love. Double the blessings. Never could I have imagined my heart expanding to this capacity. Who knew it would be two? You are joy multiplied!

To Angela Rogers, my doula—the whispers of prayers prepared me to push. The labor was intense, and you were steady ground. I will never forget that.

To Narissa Watson, my friend, my little sister, you held space no one knew about. In my process, you did not abandon me. You stayed when the terrain was rough. You saw my heart, understood the assignment, and protected our bond.

To Tori Thomas—thank you for your yes to me and for your wisdom. You are truly a gem, and I love you BIG!!

Finally, to those who stood with me in seasons of doubt, grief, and rebuilding—those who prayed, listened, encouraged, or simply stayed—thank you. Your presence mattered more than you know.

Foreword

Some stories are not written to reveal everything that happened, but to reveal what God has done. This book is one of those stories. Knowing Dawn beyond a single moment or season has been an honor while witnessing her life up close - not as a highlight reel but as a testimony marked by redemption shaped by grace, endurance, and God's restoring power.

Authoring this book required more than memory; it required wholeness. It's proof not only that she survived, but that God has healed her enough to tell the story. That, in itself, is a miracle. This book is not a "tell all" in the way the world would often define it. Instead, it is a sacred reflection of what God has done - how he redeems, restores, and repurposes even the most difficult chapters of our lives.

As you turn these pages, my prayer is that you do so with an open heart. May you see not just Dawn's journey, but the faithfulness of God woven throughout it. May this story encourage you to believe that God is still writing, still restoring, and still bringing beauty from ashes. I am grateful that Dawn said yes - to healing, to obedience, and to telling the story God entrusted to her. This book is a testimony, and I believe it will bless all who read it.

Tori C. Thomas

Introduction

"But by the grace of God I am what I am." — 1 Corinthians 15:10a

I didn't climb out of the trenches because I was strong. I was carried. There were times when I ran—from home, from myself. Moments when death whispered, and I lingered too long in its voice. Days when danger circled like vultures, seen and unseen, waiting to strike. And yet somehow, breath kept filling my lungs. Somehow, a hand I could not see kept pulling me back from edges I didn't even know I was standing on.
I remember nights when the sound of footsteps in the hall made my body lock in fear before the door even opened. And how silence became a roll of dice to what would unfold next.
Often, there were moments of pretending that everything was fine just to survive until the next thing. There was always another thing. No hope, just happenings until the next…I have deep memories of the ache of longing for my father's arms, and the sting of knowing they would never come. I have had secrets that were pressed deep into my chest. They gave a false sense of refuge from anticipated wounds that seem to have left a crumb trail back to me.

This book isn't about polished survival stories or neat, easy victories. It's about the messy, raw, and complicated journey of becoming. It's about carrying scars that still ache. It holds the process of sometimes stumbling forward when the ground shakes and finding hope in places that once looked hopeless.

If there is wisdom in these pages, healing in these lines, or strength in this voice, it isn't mine by nature. It is God's grace, poured into a woman who had nothing left to bargain with. I didn't earn rescue. I didn't even choose it well. Most days, rescue chose me.

People say that when life gives you lemons, make lemonade. I've discovered that it's not always about just lemonade. Sometimes it is the *kind* of lemonade you make. It's about the recipe you use. Do you water it down with shame? Does it come sweetened with grace? And after you've made it palatable, do you drink it alone in the dark or do you share it at a table where love and light sit with you?

My recipe comes in many flavors. God has blessed me to carry something that everyone can taste, something that everyone can be nourished by. I don't share this story because I have all the answers. I share it because silence can be heavier than words. Release comes by speaking. And maybe, just maybe my words can lift some of the silence you've been carrying.

If you have convinced yourself that brokenness is all there is, I invite you to believe differently. Brokenness is not the end of your story. Scattered across these pages are pieces of my life I once thought would destroy me. Grace has a way of gathering fragments and shaping them into something whole. My prayer is that you'll find pieces of your own story here and that hope will rise in you, even if only as a flicker at first.

This is Volume One.

Contents

Dedication iii

Acknowledgments iv

Foreword vi

Introduction vii

Chapter 1 When Home Wasn't Safe 1

Chapter 2 A Different Kind of Safe 4

Chapter 3 A New Season 7

Chapter 4 Life in a New City 13

Chapter 5 Crossroads 18

Chapter 6 Shifting Grounds 28

Chapter 7 Fractures That Spread 31

Chapter 8 Anchors and Fractures 37

Chapter 9 — A Taste of Independence 41

Chapter 10 — Cracks at Home 46

Chapter 11 — An Independent Transition 50

About the Author 57

Chapter 1 When Home Wasn't Safe

"Though my father and mother forsake me, the Lord will receive me."
— Psalm 27:10

I was a little child caught between two brothers, neither of whom had the answers I so desperately sought. My parents' marriage, though intact on the surface, was fractured in ways that weren't visible to others. What I saw at home wasn't love or care—it was tension, emotional distance, and a quiet, unspoken neglect.

Despite growing up in a house with both parents present, it never felt like home. There was no foundation of safety or trust, no solid ground to stand on. I didn't know it then, but everything that followed—every relationship, every struggle, every decision—would be shaped by the deep need to be seen, to be loved, to be valued.

My self-worth was something I didn't know how to define, much less protect. I sought validation in all the wrong places. My womanhood, my body, became tools for survival, and I didn't understand the damage I was causing to myself and others.

There were sounds I learned before I learned my times tables—the little murmur behind a door that could swell into a room, the sharp clink of a glass ashtray, the drag of a cigarette, the way the house could hold its breath. At our table, my father made games out of things that burned.

Cayenne peppers lined up like soldiers— "Who can eat the most?" he'd say, smiling like this was fun.

I would chew with water waiting, tears threatening, my mouth on fire. The room smelled like smoke—cigarettes, weed—and the buzz of alcohol hung in the air like another person in the house.

If there was laughter, I don't remember it landing. I knew where to hide. Sometimes behind the bedroom door with the loose hinge, under the blanket that didn't quite reach my toes, or in my own body—shallow breaths, a tight chest, a mind searching for exits.

Sometimes the arguments started as whispers behind a door. Then voices rose and spilled into the hallway—the kind of loud that makes a child's heart race, even if she doesn't understand the words. I didn't know what healthy love looked like, but I knew the sound of a house coming apart.

Normal is hard to remember. Trauma fogs the glass and smears the edges of what came first and what came later. Pieces come back, not always in order—like the day my brother stepped on the glass coffee table. The crack. The rush. The red. I don't remember the hospital, only the floor tilting under me.

Back then I would have told you I was fine. Children wear "fine" like armor. But I carried the house with me—the hush before the shouting, the sting of peppers, the smell of smoke, the way fear teaches you to listen for footsteps. Although these are fragmented memories, there are physical scars on my face that remind me that I survived something very real.

I often hear the words "You are so beautiful." Honestly, I agree, mostly. On other days, I see the aftermath.

I didn't understand God then, but later I would look back and trace a hand I couldn't see at the time. When I say, "the Lord will receive me," I don't say it like a slogan. I say it like someone who didn't have a safe place to land—and somehow landed anyway.

I remember once running to hide under the bed to escape a moment. I found myself pressed by my father's foot and the box spring across my chest. I couldn't move. He found the length of wire from the window screen and swung—once, twice, again. Strikes crossed my face like streaks of fire. I remember going numb, the sound of my own breath shrinking. I went to a place in my mind that I sometimes still go.

Another day, the burner on the stove glowed the color of warning. My father took my brother's hand and lowered it toward the coil. Close enough to burn, not long enough to scar. The hiss. The flinch. The cry. I stood with a frozen prayer in my throat, hoping I wouldn't be next.

Fear learned my name in those moments, and I learned how to be still.

Eventually, everything changed. The abuse became too much for anyone to ignore. My brothers and I were taken from my parents and placed in the custody of our grandparents.

These moments marked the beginning of my journey.

Chapter 2 A Different Kind of Safe

"God sets the lonely in families." — Psalm 68:6

Although I was physically removed from pain, the emotional scars remained. My grandparents did their best, but I was a child carrying trauma far beyond my years. Wounds don't heal just because the location changes.

What I remember first is the smell of my grandparents' home. There was always something good cooking, with air that felt like comfort. Three of my mother's siblings still lived in the house. One brother and two sisters. There was plenty of love to go around.

My uncle was hilarious. Sometimes, he'd hide in the hallway, jump out to scare us, and laughed until we chased him down. My aunts folded us into everyday life like it was the most natural thing in the world.

My grandfather had a way with words, turning them into music and nicknames that stuck. He gave my baby brother a name that still makes us laugh: Doom-a-loom Doom Doom. For short, he called him Doom-a-loom. The delight in his voice made the name part of our family soundtrack.

My grandmother spoke the language of love: Acts of Service. She poured out herself in home cooked meals that contained warmth, flour, sugar, and time. She baked 7UP pound cakes glazed with a delectable lemon icing, sliced warm and shared like celebration. Her homemade biscuits were clouds split open and filled with salty ham, served with red-eye gravy and syrup. On school mornings, bacon, egg, and cheese sandwiches wrapped in foil carried me into the day with the smell of home.

Christmas there felt like wonder. My favorite ornament was a pair of turtledoves that sang when you pulled the string. The tune is still in me. That year I cried because I felt like I got everything I wanted, not just gifts but a sense of belonging. While I cannot sing the tune, I still hold the memory of that turtledove ornament.

We went to church as a family. The church had a Sunshine Band and Youth Choir that we soon joined. I loved everything about it! Their house had rhythm—chores, meals, bedtime prayers. It wasn't perfect, but it was predictable. It felt like a blanket I could wear forever.

Periodic trips to the country brought hook cheese, rag bologna, crackers, and the smell of earth mixed with sunshine. For a while, I let myself be only a child.

Still, visits with my parents tugged at me. My father's presence felt blurred, like smoke, there, but not enough to hold onto. Every now and then, he'd come to pick us up to take us to his home. I would notice the tension between my grandmother and him. It could have been because his visits seemed few. Maybe it was how he managed his family. It could have been a combination of both. Still, he was daddy and I was happy to see him whenever he showed up.

During visits with my mother, the moments were clearer: playing outside with neighborhood kids, climbing dirt hills, plucking honeysuckle stems for a drop of sweet gold, and eating the berries off the blackberry bushes. I always wished I could stay longer.

Being without my mom and dad was rough. Even though the things that happened to us were harsh, the love that I had for them never left. They were my parents.

Becoming victims of abuse and being removed from our parents required counseling sessions. I didn't see the need to re-live why we were taken away. I was ready to live my new life. Safety gave me permission to exhale. I never felt the need to look over my shoulder with my grandparents. For once, I didn't feel fear as if my life were on the line.

When I became an adult, my grandfather passed away, I held my grandmother tighter. We made new memories. We'd talk on the phone and watch old television shows, laughing together as if we were in the same room. She taught me how to make skillet bread on the stovetop, and she always called me by my middle name.

She would eat rutabagas and meatless spaghetti. Sometimes she would say" Chile!" "I'm so hungry I could lick the sweat off of a cafe window!" I would yell "WHAT!" and we would burst out in laughter. Our bond lived in those small, ordinary moments that turned sacred with time.

Chapter 3 A New Season

After a while, we eventually moved back in with my mom. While the memories of what happened still lingered, the love I carried for my parents blurred some of the sharpness. A yearning that had lived inside me for so long finally quieted—we were home with my mother. I was around ten years old, and for the first time in a long while, I felt a sense of wholeness.
My father wasn't present, but I at least had most of the pieces.

The neighborhood came alive with friends my age. Some days we played in their yards, some days we tackled the dirt hill behind the duplexes, and sometimes we wandered to the bushes where berries and honeysuckles grew. We would pluck until there was little left.

Even with the joy of being home, my father stayed close in my thoughts. I missed him in small ways—a voice calling my name, arms to run into, a laugh I could memorize. I remembered how he once caught a baby robin for me. Sometimes I searched for him in crowds, half-expecting to turn a corner and see him there. As a child, I didn't understand the grown-up reasons why life had taken him a different direction. I only knew I wanted him. In time, the truth settled in. I don't remember seeing him again. The wanting didn't stop, but it learned how to stay quiet.

Still, that season held its joy. We invented games in the street, that were reminiscent of a popular video game. Kids with bikes were the main character of the game and the ones without were ghosts chasing them down. My brothers and boys from the neighborhood threw themselves into building go-karts from scraps, testing them in front of the house and laughing when things went sideways. My mom seemed lighter then—playing cards with neighborhood women, hosting spades tournaments, and laughing like a girl again. For a little while, life felt easier.

Then came the man who would become my mother's second husband. At first, he was generous, the kind of man who bought each of us our own bike. My older brother got a 10-speed, my baby brother got a dirt bike and, and I got a yellow-and-white one with a thick seat. To me it was mostly sunshine yellow. That bike was freedom. Suddenly, I was no longer one of the "ghosts" in our street game—I became one of the main characters flying through the street with the wind on my face. I loved riding up and down the block, believing—even for a moment—that I was unstoppable.

The Hill and the Ramp

Behind my mom's duplex was a hill that, to us kids, felt like a mountain. A dirt slope, mostly bare, with trees lined up at the top like guards. A chain-link fence ran across the crest, separating us from the apartments beyond. That hill wasn't just dirt—it was an adventure.

Climbing it was half the fun, a test of grit. At the top, you could see rooftops stretch out beneath you, as if you'd conquered the whole neighborhood. And in a way, we had. We waged mud-ball wars, climbed trees, and slid down on cardboard scraps until our jeans turned brown with dirt.

The boys were always searching for the next thrill. One day, it was a go-kart built from a crate and wagon wheels. Another day, a bike ramp made from old wood and loose bricks. They'd set it up in the middle of the sidewalk, away from cars, and take turns launching themselves higher and higher. I'd circle on my sunshine-yellow bike, watching.

I wasn't much for tea parties. I liked dolls well enough, but I loved dirt under my nails, wind in my face, and the kind of danger that makes your chest feel alive. I wanted to be part of the ramp-jumping crew. But every time I rolled close, courage failed me. I'd circle away, heart pounding, not ready yet.

Then came the day I told myself that it was now or never. I pedaled hard from the dead end, turned onto the sidewalk while repeating, "You can do it! You can do it! You can do it!" My bike picked up more speed than what was meant to. It was the kind of speed that was met with instant regret. I wasn't ready. I panicked. I wanted this to be over. A million thoughts were taunting me. By the time fear hit, it was too late. I was already airborne.

For a single, suspended moment, I felt like I was flying. High enough to skim the treetops. High enough to believe I could touch the sky. My heart thundered, my hands slipped with sweat against the handlebars, and I thought, I've just killed myself.

When I landed, I wasn't hurt or bruised. I probably set a record. By God's mercy, I didn't die. What broke instead was my beloved yellow sunshine. The handlebars stripped on impact, bent beyond repair. My bike was finished. I was devastated. The loss was more than wheels—it was my freedom, my pride, my joy. Losing it felt like losing a piece of myself. I never jumped another ramp after that. Truthfully, I can't remember ever having another bike.

Sometimes God gives us brief seasons of sweetness before the storm—not to erase the past or promise an easy future, but to remind us that joy still exists. Those moments become strength when the road gets harder. Children live this truth better than anyone. Even while carrying silent burdens, they still find ways to laugh, to play, to dream. Looking back, I think that's why some of us survived what should have broken us—because deep down, we still carried that quiet resilience that was secretly married to hope.

Of course, we were still just a normal family. We got into mischief, got punished, went to school, and did all the things kids do. I was in fifth grade, nearly eleven. I did not like school much and never quite felt like I fit in. I learned to navigate the halls, my peers, and my teacher. I DID NOT LIKE HER! As a matter of fact, I can still see her and that blue dress she seemed to favor.

Around that time, life shifted again. My mom remarried the man who was always around. We weren't informed about that change. There was no wedding or announcement, just someone who started visiting and soon moved in. Quietly but unmistakably, life began to move in a new direction.

My life in Memphis was becoming a past before I could identify a future.

Gentle Bridge into Chapter Four

Thank you for turning the page. We will keep walking—slowly, honestly. The next part begins with a move, the kind that seems small at first but ends up changing everything. When you're ready, come with me.

Before we move forward, I want to prepare you: the pages ahead are heavier. They hold moments of pain and confusion, and they may stir memories of your own. Please read slowly. If you need to pause, do so. Step away, breathe, and return when you're ready.

You're not reading this alone—I'm right here with you. This story doesn't end in darkness. Even here, it bends toward hope.

A short prayer:
God, I need You to meet me in this moment.
I need You to settle me in my mind and establish my thoughts.
 Steady my breath.
Hold me as I exhale.
Expand my lung capacity to inhale deeply.
 Heal what hurts.
 Honor what is true.
 Lead me gently forward.

Chapter 4 Life in a New City

Nashville was quiet in a way Memphis never was. Fewer houses, more sky and two stepbrothers. Nights felt bigger there—pond breathing behind the house, pear tree standing like it needed TLC while crickets stitched the darkness together. In hindsight, there was a different presence in the area. The pear tree yielded rotten fruit. The pond didn't offer serenity. It appeared peaceful. Up close it painted the picture of disparity. Our two-story yellow-and-brown home should have felt like a fresh start, but the silence made every feeling louder. We had space, but not our people.

Inside, everything was reset - new rooms, new rules, new rhythms. I learned the house by sound—the door that stuck in summer, the stairs that tattled every time you tried to sneak, the way voices carried from downstairs. We were starting over in a place that did not know our names. I wanted to belong here, but deep down I knew peace could be fragile.

New Surroundings

Like any move, there was that first slow look around. The air felt still, stretched out and empty. One neighbor was an elderly woman, and the nearest kid lived way down the road. His family had animals—so many. It felt like a small farm. I saw my first quail there.

My baby brother and that boy clicked instantly "Ebony and Ivory," inseparable from the start. For me, it was lonelier. Back home, I loved to run races and usually won, but here, I had no one to race. Without a crowd of neighborhood kids, I felt hidden, like a family tucked away off the map.

I started sixth grade as a new kid, at a new school, in a new city.

The Lunchbox Fight

Getting ready for school was challenging. After my mother helped me with my clothes and hair, my brothers and I walked to the school bus stop. There was no first day ride in the car that I remembered. When the big yellow bus came, I got on and immediately wanted off. The exchange of looks was my first clue I didn't belong. I carried a metal lunchbox of my favorite doll with matching thermos. I still own a replica of the doll. I wore a blue dress and my thick hair in long pigtails. I looked as if I was stepping out of an old country sitcom. The kids saw it too. I wanted to evaporate.

Once inside the school, I noticed it was predominantly black. The kids carried themselves tougher, like they had lived more life than me already. Maybe it was just my lens as the outsider, but even their laughter sounded like a dare. The looks on their faces asked, "What are you doing here? And deep down, I wondered the same.

I did my best to blend in. I made a few acquaintances after a couple of weeks. One day at recess, I lost the diamond ring my mom had given me. A small stone, but real. I was devastated. I searched everywhere. I never found it. As an adult, whenever I lose or misplace something, I will hold on to the thought of finding it for what seems like forever. I often check places that have been cleared, hoping that the lost thing would somehow show up. It's funny how habits and behavior traits follow you. I think someone found it. If that was the case, it wasn't going to be returned.

Everybody became suspects. Losing that ring put me in a space where closure never came. My mother gave me my first diamond! Who doesn't love diamonds? I was left longing. I had to go home without it. I don't quite remember what my mother's reaction was. It didn't really matter. I was without it and heartbroken. Shortly after this, a rumor spread: someone wanted to fight me.

Fear wrapped itself around me. Anxiety and I became friends in a short while. After lunch, two girls walked with me upstairs. "She said to meet her in the bathroom," one whispered. My stomach dropped and the sweat began to form. I've never been one to run away from confrontation, but this was different.

Walking that hallway felt like walking to instant doom. My lunchbox dangled from my hand, the only thing I had to hold. The bathroom was packed with girls, taller than me, watching. The way my imagination is set up, they appeared to be hanging from the ceiling and taking up every breathable space in that tiny area.

The one who wanted to fight stood in my face and shoved me hard. I stumbled into a stall and landed on the toilet. I tried to gather myself. I came out and shoved her back. It paled in comparison to what she did. Then it happened again. I landed the same way. This time my mind was racing. This girl was going to kick my butt. I'm asking myself what I could have done to get this kind of attention. I don't know *anybody* here.

Time seemed to slow down while my mind was contemplating my next action. It was fight or fold. I stood, shoved the stall door open, and pushed her back. She didn't move. She shoved harder. When I went through the stall door once more, I clicked. This time, something broke loose in me. I opened the door and swung that lunchbox with all my strength. Metal against scalp.

The crack was loud—like thunder. Gasps, screams, and in seconds, the bathroom cleared. Girls scattered. All that was left was me, my favorite doll lunchbox on one side of the room, the thermos rolling across the tile, and the handle still gripped in my hand.

She ran out, holding her head, wailing. We faced consequences. Oddly enough, it was nothing serious. Maybe the teachers felt that somehow the girl was asking for what she got, By the time I got back to class, the news had beat me there.

"Lunchbox!" they shouted.

And just like that, the new girl wasn't invisible anymore.

The nickname stuck. It followed me down hallways and onto the bus—sometimes a chant, sometimes a warning. I wasn't invisible anymore, but being noticed isn't the same as belonging. A couple of girls started saving me a seat at lunch and boys noticed me. I noticed them too. Teachers looked at me differently—some cautious, some curious.

I didn't feel brave. I just felt… allowed. Allowed to take up an inch more space than yesterday. Allowed to breathe without bracing for the next shove. The ring was still gone, but so was the version of me who thought blending in would be enough. New city, new school, new rules. I learned them fast.

The bus let us off in front of a small convenience store. That spot became the marker between school life and home life, the line I crossed every day with mixed feelings.

Once home, the house had rhythms. Some nights were not as heavy. With laughter bouncing off walls, tv humming low, everyone would move around like we knew the steps to the same dance. Other nights, the air shifted heavy and sharp, like you could cut it just by breathing wrong.
Chores kept me busy. Dishes, sweeping, wiping counters. Ordinary things. But ordinary wasn't always peace. It felt more like walking a tightrope, trying not to slip. At school, "Lunchbox" gave me space to be seen, even if it meant being a mirage. At home, silence was my shield.

Chapter 5 Crossroads

On the days when my mom and stepdad weren't home, the house felt lighter. My brothers, stepbrothers, and I would laugh together, cracking jokes, copying dance moves, and blasting familiar music. For a little while, the tension that usually lingered seemed to fade. We were just kids, trying to carve out pockets of fun inside a situation that often felt forced.

But calm never lasted long.
After the lunchbox fight a boy from the popular crowd at school took interest in me. I felt like somebody. He and his cousin were known as a tough group and whoever was on their arm became celebrities. I made friends with one of the girls.
 My new status had me stealing time for lingering conversations, a special kiss under the stairs and moments to just be. I thought it was love.

One morning, as I got off the school bus, my boyfriend and his crew were waiting for me. His face was tight, his words sharp. He had heard I was spreading a rumor that he had herpes. My heart dropped. It wasn't true, but the way he looked at me told me I had to deal with it immediately. I promised him I'd get to the bottom of it and stormed into the building.

Upstairs, I found his cousin's girlfriend, the girl I had been friendly with. I asked her straight out why she lied on me. She denied it. I asked again. This time, she cursed me out. Something in me snapped. Before I knew it, desks were screeching across the floor, hair was being yanked, and my fists were flying. I'll never forget the sickening feeling when my knuckles connected with her eye, almost like I could feel it roll beneath my skin. Teachers rushed in, pulling us apart.

We were in the middle of achievement tests that week, but none of that mattered. By this time, I was labeled a troublemaker. Both of us were suspended for six days.

My mother and stepfather came to pick me up in their pickup truck. I sat between them, shrinking smaller with every mile. My mother's hand flew out now and then to pop me—quick bursts of pain that reminded me what was waiting at home.

When we arrived, she took me upstairs to her bedroom. The air was thick. It felt like rage. She grabbed a thick yellow extension cord; the kind used on construction sites and whipped me again and again. Each lash cut through me with fire, leaving a pain far deeper than the sting on my skin. This didn't feel like discipline. It felt personal. By the time it was over, she sent me back downstairs. As I stepped onto the stairs, one last strike landed across my back. I leapt the remaining steps in desperation, my body aching, my heart pounding.

Suspension at home was its own sentence: endless chores, silence, and walking on eggshells that felt like glass. I was sore from the fight, sorer from the whipping, and determined not to stir up more trouble.

When I returned to school, things were shaky. The girl and I were no longer friends. My boyfriend and I were on thin ice. I felt both bruised and exposed.

And then, the shift began at home. My mother's husband started showing me small acts of favoritism—but only when she wasn't around. An extra plate of food. A candy bar. A bag of chips. "Don't tell nobody, "He'd whisper, as if these little gifts were secrets meant just for us.

At eleven years old, I didn't see the danger. I thought maybe he was trying to bond with me in a fatherly way. I was the only girl in a house full of boys, and in my young mind, it made sense. I accepted the treats. I kept the secrets.

What I didn't understand then was that secrecy plants roots. And secrets, even the ones wrapped in candy wrappers, carry weight too heavy for a child to bear.

Reflection:
As I look back to these moments, what stands out is how quickly innocence can be chipped away. A fight at school, whispers in the hallway, a rumor that did not belong to me. It all spiraled into consequences I could not escape. At home, punishment wasn't measured or balanced. Instead, it was fueled by anger-- sharp and merciless.

Honestly, many of us carry scars from childhood that no one sees. Some are scars from words, from silence and even from punishments that crossed a line. But scars aren't proof of defeat. They're proof you lived through it. And if you lived through it, you can heal from it.
If you are reading this and something in my story feels too close to home, I challenge you to pause and breathe deeply and purposefully.
Relax your jaws. Holding your breath makes you tense. I am right here with you.
You are not alone. Your scars are not shameful, they are survival and survival is not the end of your story. Healing is still possible.

My stepfather started spending more time downstairs. Sometimes he'd cook and eat in the den while watching TV. One night, while the boys were upstairs, he came down to prepare a homemade burger and hand-cut fries. I know because he came into my room to offer me some. I didn't realize that accepting was the doorway into something I would remember for the rest of my life.

It began quietly. No warning, no shouting, no eruption could prepare me for what was about to happen. My mother's second husband took from me what I could never get back. The violation wasn't loud. It lived in silence, behind closed doors, where shadows pressed heavier than safety.

The air grew thick. My chest tightened. Every part of me sounded an alarm I didn't know how to answer. He touched what was never his to touch. My body froze. My voice hid. It wasn't only my body that was harmed, it was the trust I thought home was supposed to give.

When it happened again, something in me shifted. I thought it was my fault. Whatever I did to ask for it, why didn't he correct me? I replayed the moments continuously in my mind. I wondered if my silence had been permission. Shame whispered lies, and I believed them. The third attempt brought the insult of a bribe—a bag of chips, as if my dignity could be bought. A voice, from inside the layers of the empty place emerged and said no more.

That's when I learned how easily innocence could be twisted. A child's hunger for attention was mistaken for agreement. A moment of quiet confusion used as consent. I didn't know how to fight back, so I went silent. But silence did not erase it. I couldn't wash it away. I could still smell it. It clung to me like a stain.

After that, I pulled inward. On the outside, I was still a sixth grader going to class; inside, I was unraveling. I didn't want to be at home, but nowhere else felt safe either. My thoughts spiraled: What if I was pregnant? Would anyone notice? Could they smell it on me? Should I tell my mother? Would she believe me?

He began avoiding me, but I could feel his fear that I might tell, fear of what my brothers or my mother might do, fear of what would happen to him. The whole house held its breath, pretending nothing had happened while everything had changed. I learned the floors, the doors, the pauses on the stairs. I learned to move in ways that kept the surface calm.

I hated him.

Even with all the noise at home, I felt like I was trapped inside my own silence. My self-image was hollow. I didn't have anyone I could talk to—not my brothers, not my mother, not my friends, not any adult I could trust. Shame locked me in. I was alone, and I didn't know what to do with myself.

The weight grew heavier every day. I heard a million voices asking questions Why me? Why couldn't I escape the smell, the memory, the stain? My chest stayed tight with guilt and fear as I relived those moments repeatedly.

Eventually, I convinced my mother to let me go back to Memphis and live with my grandparents. When she said yes, I didn't hesitate. Leaving my brothers tore at me, but staying felt like suffocation.

At my grandparents' house, life slowed. I repeated sixth grade under their protective wing. For a short while, I could breathe a bit easier. That structure, safety, and love in the way they knew how to give was a familiar space minus two. But peace didn't erase memories. It didn't soothe the longing I carried—for my siblings, for my mother, for a family that felt whole. I didn't know how to process the rollercoaster of emotions.

Even though distance gave me room to fully exhale, it didn't erase what had been done. The trauma stayed with me, clinging to me like my skin, even in a safe place.

Brain Break — A Pause for Healing ✦

Looking back, I know what I couldn't have understood at eleven: none of it was my fault. I was a child. A daughter. A little girl who should have been safe in her own home.

But shame has a way of making you forget who you are. It whispers lies until you think they're the truth—that you asked for it, that you deserved it, that no one would believe you anyway. And for years, even into adulthood, I carried those lies like they were stitched into my soul like clothing.

Healing didn't come overnight. It took time, counseling, prayer, and a whole lot of grace. I had to relearn how to breathe without guilt filling my lungs. I had to face the memories instead of running from them. And slowly, God began to peel back the layers of humiliation and self-disdain I had never asked to wear. I've learned that "ING" is a present state. It's not final at all. And now, I'm heal-ING. I'm surrender-ING. God is teach-ING
And I'm yet learn-ING.

If you've ever carried the weight of someone else's sin against you, hear me: you are not what happened to you. It may have marked you, but it does not define you.

Your voice still matters. Your worth is still intact. Your life still holds purpose.

There is life after silence. There is healing after harm. And yes, there is joy waiting, even for you.

While I sought the comfort of my grandparents, even they couldn't erase the ache. I missed my siblings, my mother, the pieces of family I still longed to hold together. The distance gave me room to breathe, but it didn't untangle the memories I carried or the silence that clung to me.

That season didn't last. Before long, I was back in Nashville And while my family was living in a different house and different neighborhood, the same unrest was waiting at the door.

Life inside those walls didn't soften. If anything, the arguments between my mother and her husband grew sharper, heavier. One night, I was so afraid he might really hurt her that I held my breath, bracing for the worst. That was the last fight of that kind, because soon after, we packed up and moved again.

This time, it was just my mother, my brothers, and me.

The new place was a duplex complex still under construction. We were the very first tenants in our unit, and for a moment the smell of fresh paint and the feeling of clean floors made it seem like life was being reset. No stepfather. No chaos from fights. Just us.

But new walls didn't mean erasure of past habits. My mother went back to working long shifts, sometimes overnight, sometimes changing from week to week, which left us alone often. My oldest brother, already a teenager, started carving out his own space in bold and reckless ways. My baby brother and I leaned on each other, sometimes well, sometimes not. Mischief became our glue.

That summer, the neighborhood turned into our playground. The kids were mostly boys, some of my brother's age, some closer to mine—but I ran right alongside them. We played chase when the streetlights went off, hiding in the cover of the night. There were times we would wander down to the creek, coming back with buckets of tadpoles and crawfish, proud of our little trophies.

Inside, I was learning new kinds of freedom. With my mother gone so much, there was no one hovering. That duplex was where I tried cooking for the first time. I remember burning a piece of chicken so badly it turned black as coal. We laughed, but deep down I was proud—I had tried.

Of course, my brothers pushed boundaries further. When my mother slept, my oldest brother sometimes slipped away with her car. Once, he convinced me to ride along. My hands shook the whole time, fear pressing against my chest harder than the seatbelt. I didn't want to crash, I didn't want to get caught—but he was wild, living on the edge. I only rode with him once. That was enough. I never told on him, but I knew I couldn't stomach that thrill again.

Not all our mischief was harmless. Ding-dong ditch. Smearing nasty things on doorknobs. Sneaking into a neighbor's house when no one was home—not to steal, just to raid the kitchen and leave like nothing had happened. Reckless. Dangerous. But at the time, it felt like fun.

The duplex carried both laughter and shadows. That's where the nightmares began. They didn't come every night, but often enough that I dreaded closing my eyes.

Sometimes the dreams replayed what had already happened, the weight of his body, his hands, and the fear that froze me. Other times, they twisted into shapes worse than memory, leaving me breathless and soaked in sweat. Sleep should have been refuge, but instead, it became another battlefield.

The walls of that duplex held a silence that was too loud for me to escape. Even when the day was full of noise, night reminded me of what I had lived through. My memories kept my mental archive section current.

Chapter 6 Shifting Grounds

The tension in that duplex only grew heavier. Maybe it was the strain of my mother trying to do it all alone, maybe it was just the way life had always been with us—but the walls didn't shelter me. They pressed in, closer every day, until eventually, I couldn't take it anymore.

I packed a few of my mother's clothes—hers looked better than mine, and in my young mind, they symbolized a version of a life I longed for but couldn't reach. Shame clung to me, nightmares stalked me, and silence smothered me. I needed out.

A classmate helped me run. We ended up in a dimly lit house with strangers. She had her own distractions, and I was left sitting in a corner, wide-eyed and restless. I couldn't sleep. Couldn't relax. Fear followed me like a shadow, and even in that crowded house, I had never felt more alone.

The escape didn't last. We were caught at a fast-food restaurant, sipping coffee when we should have been at school. That was the first time I ever rode in the back of a police car. It wasn't handcuffs or flashing lights that broke me—it was the humiliation of being paraded home like a runaway stray.

But walking back into that house didn't bring relief. My brothers told me in hushed voices what my mother had prepared while I was gone: three oversized pillows stacked high and a metal pipe set aside. The plan was cruel and simple—smother the evidence under the pillows, then strike without leaving marks.

I stood in disbelief. I had run away searching for safety, for love, for some sign that I mattered. Instead, my return was met with punishment, as if I were nothing more than another problem to be solved.

At thirteen, was it rebellion? Or was it survival? I still don't know. What I do know is that I was carrying a weight far too heavy for a child to bear. And coming home to that kind of reception only made the load heavier—so heavy that I wondered how much longer I could carry it.

The silence in me finally cracked open one day. My mother saw my distance, my exhaustion, my rebellion simmering under the surface. She didn't see the root of it—only the symptoms. Words flew between us, sharp and angry. I hadn't planned to speak, but suddenly it all erupted out of me.

"I CAN'T SLEEP BECAUSE I'M HAVING NIGHTMARES! HE DID THIS TO ME! HE DID THIS TO ME!"

The room froze. My brothers stared, wide-eyed. My mother's face shifted—disbelief, confusion, anger—before she moved. She grabbed me, shoved me into the bathtub, and her hands wrapped around my throat.

I remember the cold enamel against my back, the shock of air leaving my lungs, my body thrashing as if on its own. Seconds felt like hours. I wasn't being disciplined, I was being silenced. I thought I might die there, not from the secret I carried, but from the hands of the one I had finally told. Whatever the amount of trust that I had in my mother vanished. The trail that indicated it was once there was labeled regret.

Her reaction ended when her boyfriend—the man who would later become her third husband—pulled her off me. I lay there coughing, gasping, shaking. Alive, but shattered. And more certain than ever, my voice was dangerous. The space that should have welcomed my tears and embraced my shattered pieces left me with a wound so deep that infection settled in and affected everything I did or thought.

Chapter 7 Fractures That Spread

The next thing was the system. Once the truth was spoken, the authorities had to be called. The police, the reports, the questions, all became part of my life. Telling my mother was hard, but telling strangers was worse. I had to relive every detail: what happened, when it happened, where it happened. The words were pulled out of me like threads unraveling a garment, leaving me exposed. It wasn't about healing—it was about evidence.

There was counseling, interviews, and the possibility of court. I was just a child, but suddenly my voice had to carry the weight of proof. Every time I spoke, I wondered if they believed me, if my story would matter, or if it would get lost in the shuffle of papers and legal words I didn't understand. The system was supposed to protect me, but instead, it made me feel like I was the one on trial.

All of this happened while the divide between my siblings and me widened. Somewhere in the shuffle, my oldest brother was sent back to Memphis to live with our father. I believe it was because the testosterone was too heavy between my mother's new man and her son who was becoming a man. Maybe the competition for her attention was more than she was willing to deal with.

Whatever the reason, I felt it deeply. He had always been a part of the noise, the laughter, the fights, the survival. Now he was gone. Without him the house felt emptier, like someone had pulled a thread loose in our fabric and the whole thing unraveled. Even now, that split still shows. We love each other, be we aren't as close as we might have been. His story unfolded one way and ours in another. I longed for him. Not just because I missed him, but because I needed him. He was my big brother. I needed someone who knew me, someone who could stand with me in all of this. Instead, I felt split in unequal units: part of me trying to survive home life, part of me dragged through courts and counseling rooms, and another part grieving the family that kept slipping further away.

The courtroom was another kind of battlefield. I thought telling my mother was the hardest thing I'd ever done, but I was wrong. Now I had to tell strangers, officials, and lawyers the same story repeatedly. Each time I felt like being I was stripped of another layer of myself.

The court liaison tried to explain what would happen, how the questioning would go, but their words were like another language. Jargon I couldn't understand. My stomach churned, my insides jackhammered like concrete, and the embarrassment burned so hot I wished I could have morphed into another life.

They asked me what happened. They asked me to repeat it. They asked me to describe details I didn't want to remember. And then they asked what he was wearing. That memory, etched forever in my mind, made me want to crawl out of my own skin. I was only a child, but I was being forced to carry an adult's burden in front of my mother, in front of strangers, in front of a system that didn't know how much it was costing me just to speak.

My mother did what she thought was right—she pressed charges, she fought for justice by following protocol. As her daughter, I needed more than an appointment keeper. I needed her arms, her presence, her nearness. And she did not provide it. Maybe she didn't know how to give me what I truly yearned for...Her. Whether it was her own fear, her own pain, or just her not knowing what I needed, the result was the same: I felt like the other woman in my own mother's house.

I have never felt so dirty. So low. Divided. My body was budding into womanhood, my hormones shifting, my mind flooded with questions about desire and shame. Why me? Why did my body react the way it did? Why did his attention make me feel like I had done something to invite it? The violation planted questions in me that I wasn't ready to ask, much less answer.

I was in a million pieces, and every piece had a voice. Some screamed shame. Some whispered confusion. Others stayed silent, buried under the weight of carrying too much too soon.

After all the prepping, the meetings, the counseling sessions, and the fragile hope that maybe—just maybe—justice would come, I found myself in that courtroom. I was only eleven when it happened, but every question made me feel like I was the one on trial. His attorney's voice was sharp, his questions twisted. They weren't just about that night, or the bribe of chips, or the robe I'll never forget—they went after my life, my family, even things that had nothing to do with what was taken from me.

I remember the way the judge looked at me, the way the jury looked at me, the way I felt like every eye was measuring me, not him. The words got tangled in my head, and no matter how I tried to answer, it felt like I was already guilty of something. Guilty of existing. Guilty of telling. Guilty of being there at all.

I felt angry. I felt sarcastic. I felt lonely. I felt abandoned. I felt disregarded. I felt vulnerable. I felt unseen. I felt unheard. More than anything, I just wanted to crawl into someone's arms and be a little girl again, safe and sheltered.

But instead, I had to point at him— "Yes, Your Honor, that's him"— and then sit there while the weight of it all pressed down on me. After all the details, after all the courage it took to name what happened, the verdict came: mistrial.

Nothing.

All the tears, all the fear, all the humiliation of repeating what I wished I could forget, it ended with nothing. —
 I felt like dust scattered on the wind—no form, no weight, no worth.
But in the middle of that silence, there was my baby brother. He didn't have the words—how could he? We were both just kids, trying to understand a world that didn't make sense. But what he did have was presence. His laughter in the small moments, his company when the nights felt too heavy, his ability to just be there kept me tethered when everything else seemed determined to pull me apart.

The system had failed me. The adults who were supposed to know what to do had left me exposed. But my brother's nearness reminded me I wasn't completely alone. We fought like siblings, we laughed like siblings, but beneath it all, he became the one person onto whom I could hold. Even if he didn't know it, he was my lifeline.
After the mistrial, life didn't quiet down. It grew heavier and thicker. The system called for another round. Another trial, another set of attorneys, counselors, and another attempt at justice. It felt like less protection and more exposure. By then, I was fourteen. My oldest brother came up briefly to meet with attorneys and speak on my behalf. I wanted that visit to draw us closer, but it left a bigger divide and his presence was fleeting. We he left, another part of me left too.
During that time, we were living with my mother's boyfriend. My mother, under the weight of his expectations, tightened her grip that landed mostly on me. If he had a complaint, we felt the fallout. The pressure was suffocating.
Counselling didn't feel like a safe place anymore. I could no longer trust that whatever I shared was confidential. The conversations somehow became available to my mother and her boyfriend. Words that were supposed to help me were thrown back at me with fire. Where could I

run? Where could I breathe? I carried my indignity in silence and wore the cloak of it like it was sealed on me at birth.

By then, my life felt like a thousand-pound weight was strapped to my chest. Normal teenage moments were poisoned. I still had desires that were awakening within. I had questions and feelings that came with growing into womanhood. They became tangled with guilt, confusion, and memories I couldn't wash away. I hated the way I looked, and I hated the way people looked at me in the court room. I felt hyper exposed to the older opposite sex population. The questions were relentless. I was reminded that no matter how many times I told my truth, it didn't seem to matter.

And then came my breaking point.

I was tired. Soul tired. From the outside I might have looked like a mere troubled teenager but on the inside, I felt like an old soul worn down by years of pain packed into too few years of living. My life felt like one big ball of nothing. No safe place, no trust, no peace. One day, I decided that I was done. I no longer wanted what life was offering. All it had done was take. It took so much that the small moments of laughter were no longer worth it.

I had access to a big bottle of aspirin. I took them all and waited. I didn't know how long it would take. I just wanted to go quietly. No last conversations. No notes. No protest, just gone. I laid down in my bed in silence. I anticipated the end. I waited for it. I don't remember falling asleep, I do, however, remember waking up to the same life I tried to leave. I didn't realize it then, but it was God's hand holding me. Even in my attempt to give up, He refused to let me go.

Maybe you've found yourself in the kind of place where the weight feels too heavy, when your soul feels tired or when the thought of not being here feels easier than facing another day. If that's you, hear me: Your pain is real but so is your purpose. The enemy would love you to believe that your story ends here. It doesn't. You're reading this because you are here on purpose.

I know what it feels like to want to disappear. I know what it is to think there is no way forward. But I also know this: God has a way of stepping into our darkest moments to hold us when we can't hold ourselves. He whispers about life where we only hear despair. He sees you. Not just the version of you that feels broken, but also the one He created with intention, beauty, and strength.

If you are wrestling with thoughts of giving up, take a moment and breathe. Pause. Reach out to someone you trust. If you can't reach them, I pray that God puts you on their mind and they find you where you are. Write, create, and channel that energy into something beautiful. Most of all reach toward the One who calls you His own.

You may have been bruised. You may have been battered and feel broken. You're still on the potter's wheel. Just because a moment of collapse happened, doesn't mean that you are discarded. Instead, The Potter puts more water on you to mold you into what he has in mind. Life will not always feel like this. Once you give it to God and let Him take control of your process, peace will find you. Joy will find you. Grace will find you. And when it does, you will see yourself standing again—not because pain never happened but because you'll realize that you were never abandoned in the middle of it.

One day, when you look back, you'll see the very thing that threatened to end you became the place where strength started growing. God never failed me—and He won't fail you.

Chapter 8 Anchors and Fractures

Life at home was still unsettled, but in the middle of all that instability, something steady began to grow between my baby brother and me. The world around us kept shifting—houses, schools, adults in and out of our lives—but he and I became anchors for each other.

He wasn't just my little brother; he was my first real best friend. Of course, we fought like siblings do, but beneath the squabbles was an unshakable truth: when it mattered, we were in each other's corner. I knew he would go to war for me, and he knew I'd do the same for him.

We built a private world together, one only we could understand. Even now, decades later, a single phrase or even a sound can send us into laughter that feels endless. Back then, the smallest thing could turn into a thirty-minute inside joke. We once even called ourselves a rap duo—"Undercover"—scribbling rhymes like we were bound to make it big.

Often left on our own, we found ways to fill the silence. Sometimes it was harmless laughing until our stomachs hurt or exploring the neighborhood like it belonged to us. Sometimes it was trouble, the kind that only unsupervised kids can find. But no matter what, those moments stitched us together. Laughter was our glue, mischief our language.

But underneath the laughter, I carried a hollow ache. I didn't know where to place my value, so I went searching for it in the wrong places. I didn't have relationships with boys—I had encounters. Promiscuous moments that promised connection but always left me emptied. Each time, I hoped to be chosen, to be loved, and each time I was let down and left to clean up the residue of my decisions Eventually, the emptiness became so normal that I stopped expecting more.

By the eighth grade, all that hurt and confusion started spilling sideways. I became a bully—not to everyone, but enough to make my presence known. I made sure girls outside of my circle knew I was tough. I pushed others down because I didn't know how to lift myself up. Strangely, it gave me popularity and a sense of belonging I craved, but it didn't heal the emptiness. On the outside, I looked bold. On the inside, I was still the same lost, hurting girl.

By the ninth grade, skipping school became routine. Sometimes I'd stay home pretending to be sick. Other times, I'd wander to an abandoned townhouse burned so badly no one could live there anymore. Looking back, I know God's hand was on me. Anyone could have seen me slip inside. Anything could have happened. But nothing did. Even in my recklessness, God was protecting me when I didn't have the wisdom to protect myself.

I told myself I was free, making my own choices. But deep down, I was bound—by shame, loneliness, and the lies that told me I wasn't worth more. My brother and I laughed together, we explored together, but when I was alone, the silence told the truth I didn't want to face. I didn't know who I was or my place in this world.

At home, my mother was on her third marriage. She kept her world private, and we knew little of what she carried, but I felt the weight of it in her silence and in her words. Sometimes, I believed we were in her way—as if the life she wanted was just out of reach because of us.

As I got older, I felt the disappointment in her eyes like a shadow that wouldn't lift. When she looked at me, I often wondered if she only saw what had happened with her second husband—like I was a reminder of the pain she wanted to forget.

Her words confirmed my fears. In moments of anger, she said things I can never forget: "I wish I had closed my legs when you were being born." Or "You've been nothing but a disappointment your whole life." Those words cut deeper than any punishment. They weren't just about my choices or mistakes—they sliced into the core of who I was.

And yet, even as I write this, I find myself trying to defend her. Maybe she wasn't loved properly. Maybe she was carrying wounds of her own. Maybe survival shaped her in ways I'll never fully understand. It doesn't erase the hurt, but it shows the complexity of love: that you can ache for someone and ache because of them, both at once. This was my reality. My trauma.

Reflection

Words can bruise just as deeply as hands. Long after the sound fades, the echo stays. They shape how we see ourselves and how we step into the world. My mother's words did that to me. They weren't just sentences in a heated moment—they became shadows I carried, whispers I still must fight against every day.

But here's what I've learned in hindsight: those words, no matter how sharp, don't hold the final say. They don't have the power to define who we are—not unless we let them.

There is a greater voice, steady and true, that speaks over every life. A voice that calls us chosen, loved, and created with intention. The sting of rejection and disappointment may feel like it's carved into stone, but grace has a way of softening even the hardest surfaces.

Strength doesn't come from pretending the hurt never happened. It comes from daring to believe that something greater can grow in its place. The weight of rejection can crush you if you carry it alone—but with God, it becomes the soil where resilience takes root.

You are not the sum of hurtful words. You are not the disappointment someone said you were. You are the work of a God who formed you with care and purpose, shaping you for good even when everything around you feels unstable.

That truth is steady—even when everything else shifts.

Chapter 9 — A Taste of Independence

Work wasn't new to me by the time I stepped into young adulthood. I started earning paychecks at fifteen. My first job was at a famous fast-food restaurant, and then another restaurant while I was still just sixteen and in the eighth grade. Those jobs gave me an early sense of independence. By the time I reached eighteen, the rhythm of working—clocking in, serving customers, and cashing a check—was already familiar.

What I wasn't ready for, though, was the load that came with adulthood. As a teenager with a job and money, I felt I had freedom to spend time attending to my needs, something that gave me a taste of belonging in a world bigger than me. But as I grew older, that same paycheck carried expectations. Bills. Responsibilities. Choices that stretched further than the weekend. It wasn't pocket money anymore, it was survival.

Employment at that age shaped me in ways I didn't recognize at the time. Not only did I learn how to work, but how to take care of myself. Even when life was unstable, I could return to the steady rhythm of earning. That rhythm became both a shield and a lifeline, helping me navigate the fragile beginnings of adulthood.

Independence was both a badge of honor and a heavy chain. I was learning to keep myself afloat without a guidebook, carrying responsibilities my shoulders weren't quite ready for. But nothing prepared me for the loss that crashed into my life that year.

News of my father's death reached me like a blow I couldn't see coming. I longed for him my whole life—for the embrace I imagined, for the relationship I dreamed of and for the sense of fatherly comfort I believed only he could give. I never stopped hoping that one day I would run into his arms, we would embrace and he would see me—not the regretted choices I came from, but his daughter. That chance was taken away.

He was gone. Just like that.
No last words.
No reconciliation.
No goodbye.

I remember running out of the house screaming, the sound of my voice strange to my own ears—like it belonged to someone else. Grief tore through me before I could even form thoughts. My body reacted before my mind could catch up.

Later, I pieced together the details. His sisters tried everything to reach us. They called radio stations, placed notices in the local newspaper, and searched for ways to find me and my baby brother. No one reached us in time. They had no choice but to move forward with the funeral arrangements. By the time we knew, he was already buried.

The numbness came after. A hollow, heavy quiet that followed me everywhere. I remember wishing I could blink it away, like a genie in a TV show—erase the finality of it all. But there was no undoing this. No last words. No final embrace. No chance to tell him the words that had burned inside me for years: I love you, Daddy.

When I learned how my father died, the grief cut even deeper. It hadn't been sudden in the way accidents take someone quickly. It was slow, cruel, the kind of end that came with sickness. He had contracted HIV through drug use, and I couldn't stop imagining the pain he must have endured. Had he been scared? Did he feel alone? Did he long for us in those last moments?

That knowledge weighed heavily on me. It wasn't just that he was gone, it was how he left. I felt robbed of time, of closure, of the chance to sit beside him and say, Daddy, I love you. The thought of him suffering without us there cut sharper and spread deeper than words could touch.

And then the questions came. Who was with him in those last hours? Was his second wife there? What about the children he had with her? What were their names? Did they know about us? Had they ever heard him talk about the family he left behind? Did they mourn him like I did, or was our part of his story tucked away in silence, a chapter he never spoke aloud?

Even now, I can feel how raw that ache was. I was left staring at the sky, wondering if he was looking back through the clouds. Sometimes I even imagined the shape of a cloud turning into his face, and I would whisper, "Daddy," as tears slid down my cheeks. But no imagining, no wondering, no questioning could fill the void of not being there, not saying goodbye, not having the chance to be loved as his daughter in the end.

Soon after his death, I moved back to Memphis with his older sister and my cousins. That season was rough in unusual ways, mostly because when I finally made it back home, he wasn't there. I sat outside often with eyes lifted to the sky, searching for him in the clouds.

It was still fresh for my aunts and uncles, and no one really wanted to talk about it, not in the way I needed. I wanted every detail, every story, anything that could help me feel like I had been there.

What I didn't understand then was that nothing could give me the comfort I longed for—because the comfort I wanted required him to still be alive. The ache grew heavy, and before long, I found myself back in Nashville.

By that time, my mom, who had been separated, moved in again with her third husband, and that became my new residence.

Daddy,

I don't know where to start, except to say I wish I had the chance to give you these words while you were here. For so long, I longed for your presence-- for a voice calling my name, for arms to run into, for the simple reassurance that I was your daughter and that mattered to you.

I hold only a few memories of us, but I've carried them all these years like treasures. I remember the baby robin you caught for me, the way you showed me something so fragile and alive. I wanted more moments like that, moments where I could say, " That's my daddy!"
Instead, what I had was silence. Absence. A longing that stretched across the years. When I finally learned you were gone, it felt like the hope that I had been clinging to, crumbled all at once. I never got to tell you how much I loved you. I never got to hear if you loved me back.

I know addiction stole pieces of you and that sickness took you without me ever really knowing you. Still, you were my father and I needed you. Decades later, I find myself wishing things had been different.
I wish I had more than scraps of memory. I wish you knew that your little girl didn't stop looking for you – that I never stopped wanting you. I'll say it now, even if the words only echo inside me: I love you daddy. I wish you could stayed long enough to hear it.

At this point in my life, you would have been a grandfather and a great-grandfather. You would have seen love, laughter, and legacy continue through me and my children. A part of me still carries you forward into every generation that came after you. I will forever miss you.

Your daughter,
Dawn

Chapter 10 — Cracks at Home

Life with my mother's third husband was up and down. He was strict—military strict—but that discipline brought a kind of order I had never known before. From him, I learned practical skills I still carry today: how to cut up a whole chicken, shuck corn, clean fish, and snap peas fresh from the garden. He showed me the rhythm of country living, where challenging work tied your hands to the earth and meals came from scratch.

Looking back, I can say he was the best husband my mother ever had. He gave her stability she had never known before, and with him, she lived a better life than what I believe she was used to. For a while, this became our "new normal."

But even with that stability, I was still carrying the weight of my father's death and adjusting to a new house, a new neighborhood, and a new rhythm of life. Home carried an undercurrent of tension that seemed to grow heavier every day. Arguments between my baby brother and my mom escalated often, while I tried my best to stay out of the crossfire. Most days, I kept to myself, hoping that if I stayed quiet, I wouldn't be pulled into it.

It worked—until one October day, everything shifted.

I was lying in bed with the radio on, trying to drown out the argument spilling through the walls. I don't remember what started it, but I do remember hearing my brother's voice shout words that chilled me:

"I hate you, and I hope you die!"

I turned the radio up, trying to block it out, but his next words still reached me:

"If you keep on, I'm going to have to tell your husband something—me and Dawn!"

The air changed instantly. The atmosphere in the house was charged, as if the walls themselves were holding their breath. Dread sank into my stomach. I knew what was coming.

My mother's voice came sharp and commanding, calling me out of my room. I froze, then heard her again, harsher this time, laced with curses: "Get out here!"

Reluctantly, I stepped into the hallway. I walked towards the den. My brother stood beside me. My mother stood across from us, pointing toward her husband, who was sitting in his chair. She demanded, "Tell him! You've got something to say? Tell him!"

And then my brother spoke the words I had never wanted anyone else to hear.

Her husband looked stunned. "What? What did you just say?" he pressed.

My brother repeated it, then turned to me. "Tell him, Dawn! Help me out!"

Everything happened so fast. At the same time, my mind was racing. I believe I had an outer body experience. At least I wanted to.

I was looking at my brother in disbelief. I'm asking questions in my head: "What are you doing?" "Why did you call my name?" I literally wanted to disappear.

I couldn't form the words. Hesitantly, I nodded. My silence was enough. In that frozen moment, everything shifted. I thought she was going to beat me up. Instead, I was met with curses, screams, and the sting of rejection. My mother unleashed her fury on me and not my brother. She began spitting words that cut deep as if I was the reason all of this was happening. Then came the final blow: "Get out of my house!"

I gathered what little I had and walked out into the night. No phone. No transportation. Nowhere to go. The October air bit into my skin as I laid down on a red blanket in the grass on the darkest side the house. We lived in the last house on a dead-end street. Our dog at the time was my only comfort and that patch of ground became my bed for nights to come.

Survival became a ritual. I slipped over to the neighbor's house at times to use the phone, or just to step inside for a little while and get out of the elements. But when the night came, I always returned to that patch of grass.
My mother didn't ask where I was. I'm not sure she cared.

Her husband though, he noticed. The next day, he let me inside briefly, trying to reason with her. I could see he wanted me to stay, but her answer was final: "Get out of my house!" Every now and then, he would slip me something to eat—a plate of food, scraps from the kitchen. But the message was clear: I was on my own. I can't remember ever crying. The building of rejection I lived in created another storage room for me. Inside, I had piles of 'thrown away.' on hand.

That season stripped me bare. The ground beneath me was cold, but the rejection was colder. I was at home—and homeless at the same time.

Being out on the side of the house felt like forever. In truth, it was only about a week, but the weight of those days pressed down like an eternity. This wasn't camping, where you expect discomfort and prepare for it. This was homelessness in its rawest form. Worse still, it was homelessness at home—a contradiction that cut deeper than the cold grass beneath me.

One neighbor let me use her phone now and then, and sometimes I lingered inside for a few minutes just to warm up and feel human again. But there was no lasting refuge.

Eventually, I reached out to a friend. Together, we made our way to her boyfriend's grandparents' house. It wasn't permanent, but it gave me a temporary roof and a bed I didn't have to share with the night air.

When the boyfriend's mother found out what had happened, she stepped in. She and her husband opened their doors to us, moving all of us into their home. My friend and her boyfriend shared a room downstairs, and I was given a small room across the hall. For the first time in what felt like forever, I had a door to close, a bed of my own, even if borrowed, and a little slice of stability.

I lived there for about a year. During that time, my baby brother sometimes drove my mother's car to see me. He didn't have much to offer, but his visits were proof that I hadn't been completely forgotten.

That season wasn't easy, but it reminded me that even scraps of kindness could mean survival.

Chapter 11 An Independent Transition

By the time most kids my age were still figuring out who they wanted to be, I was already figuring out how to survive on my own. My first real steps into independence came through a temp service that placed me wherever there was work to be done. One week it was office work, the next it was something tougher. The job that still sticks in my memory was at a car lot.
I had no idea what to expect. My friend, her boyfriend and I worked together. When we arrived at the lot, I noticed that we weren't the only ones. There were quite a few of us. Different sexes and races. I had a thought. While I was being dealt my life cards, I wasn't the only one who needed to take whatever they could get. I didn't know their story, but I knew they had to have a moment that called for this kind of solution.

As we lined up, people in charge handed us thin shammies and pointed to rows of brand-new cars. A water truck sprayed them down, and it was our job to wipe every inch until they gleamed. Roof to headlights, wheels to chrome. Not only was I cold, but I was also unprepared for the task. No gloves of any kind. Some of the people who had done the job before would offer to take turns wearing rubber ones.

While that gave some relief, by the end of the shift, my hands were raw and burning, stinging with cold, I complained but I kept wiping because I needed the paycheck. It wasn't glamorous, it was grit. That was survival. The work was grueling, but it gave me something else too: a rhythm.

No matter what situation waited where I lived, I had somewhere to go, something to do, a reason to keep moving forward. Even in the smallest paycheck, I found a piece of independence.

Eventually, I landed a job at famous theme park. Compared to the car lot, it felt like stepping into another world. I wore white shorts and a striped shirt and had a popcorn and pink lemonade cart. Although days were hot and sticky, I ran my cart with pride. Sweat ran down my back as I filled cup after cup of that sweet coolness and made fresh popcorn.

All this along with fighting off yellow jackets. There was laughter in that place that was contagious. Music floated through the air, families smiled, children pointed at rides. For the first time in a long time, I felt like I belonged to something ordinary.

On breaks, I wandered the park, exploring sections I'd never seen before. Sometimes I tried new food, sometimes I just watched people, soaking in the sense of being part of a bigger world. It was a reprieve—work, yes, but also light in the middle of my heaviness.

That's where I met him, the security guard. He seemed harmless at first, walking me to my cart, checking on me during breaks, waiting after shifts so we could walk back together. It wasn't love. It wasn't even attraction. It was a simple presence. On the days he wasn't around, I noticed the absence. I wasn't used to someone showing up just because they wanted to.

But even the good things had cracks. Work ended, as it always did, and living under other people's roofs came with its own weight. Arguments flared, frictions piled up, and one day I came home to find a note on my bed: Find somewhere else to live.

Desperate, I called the only person I could think of—the guard from the theme park. He told me to come stay with him and his girlfriend. She opened her home, and for a while, it looked safe enough. But the cracks widened. He started crossing boundaries, sneaking moments that weren't his to take, pressing for what didn't belong to him.

And when my life said that was my bargain, I gave in to the attempts. Embarrassment wrapped itself around me again, and another piece of my dignity was gone. The roof I thought might hold was collapsing. He began to be careless. He would take bold risks that compromised my safety. Their fights became my burden. I couldn't stay. I'm not sure what would've happened if I did. I had to decide on my next move.

In my desperation, I reached back toward the very place I'd been cast out of before. I called my mother's husband. I asked if I could come home. He didn't answer right away. He said he'd talk to my mother and call me back. Those moments felt like an eternity, my heart pounding in my chest. I was on the cliff. I didn't know if I was jumping, being pushed or saved

When the phone finally rang, his voice carried the answer I hadn't expected. Yes. I could come home.

Relief washed over me—not because home was safe, not because wounds had healed, but because I wasn't outside anymore. I wasn't unwanted on the curb; I wasn't sneaking through someone else's door. I was back. And even in that fragile return, I could feel something greater than myself holding me up.

I was learning that independence wasn't always about standing alone. Sometimes it was about finding the courage to reach out—even when reaching out felt like the hardest thing of all. For me, reaching out also meant another roll of the dice.

Reflection — Closing Volume One

"Returning home" was never simple for me. I didn't have a choice, it felt like my last resort. Walking back through that door meant stepping into unspoken things that still hung in the air: forgiveness that hadn't been offered, wounds that hadn't healed, and questions I didn't dare ask. It wasn't a place of rest but a place of eggshells, where every step had to be measured and careful. I didn't know what else to do, but I'm grateful that even then, mercy met me and kept me standing.

That's the truth about returning. It doesn't always feel like home. Sometimes you go back because you want to, and sometimes you go back because you must. Either way, it rarely matches the picture you held in your heart.

But there's another kind of return. One that isn't about a house or about people—it's about God. That return is different. His door is never locked. His love never says, "Get out." His presence doesn't wait until you're cleaned up, healed, or whole. It welcomes you as you are, every time.

Even when I was lying on the cold ground, even when doors stayed closed, even when I felt unwanted in my own mother's house—God still held space for me. I didn't always see it, but He was there, steady, keeping me from shattering in ways I couldn't have repaired on my own.

Maybe your story has its own kind of return. Maybe you've gone back to places or people that disappointed you. Maybe you've returned just to survive. Whatever your story looks like, know this: your truest home isn't in a building or in people who can fail you.

Your truest home is in God.

When you turn to Him—whether it's the first time or the hundredth, you won't find rejection. You will find rest. You will find open arms. You will find the kind of love that holds steady, no matter how far you've wandered or how heavy your story feels.

This is where Volume One closes, but not where the story ends. Because returning doesn't stop at survival, it leads to restoration. And that journey, the one that transforms brokenness into wholeness, still lies ahead.

A Letter to the Men

To the men who have picked up this book, let me pause and speak directly to you.
I know you carry things that most people never ask about. You've been taught to hold it all together, to be strong, to provide and to protect. Somewhere along the way, your own wounds got buried under everyone else's expectations. Just because you don't show the scars doesn't mean they aren't there.
Your story matters.
Your pain matters and so does your healing.
You matter.
You don't have to hide behind silence or keep proving your worth. You are already worthy and already loved. More importantly you are already seen by the God who made you.
I want you to know this: admitting that you hurt is not a weakness. It's courage. Letting God into those broken spaces is not failure. It's the beginning of being made whole.

Just like clay in The Potter's hands, you are still being shaped. And like a diamond, the pressure you've endured has not destroyed you. It's refining you. So, stand! Do so, not because you have anything to prove but because you are already something.

You are a man with purpose, a man with value and a man that God has not overlooked. This book carries the voice of a woman, but it also carries a message for you. You are not forgotten and you are not alone. May these words meet you where you are and remind you that you too can heal, rise and live freely.

About the Author

Dawn S. Shoats is a wife, mother, grandmother, and faith-based leader who cares deeply about healing, restoration, and becoming whole. Her life and work are rooted in service, shaped by compassion, and guided by a steady faith in God's ability to form beauty in unseen places.

Dawn has spent many years working in education and ministry, walking alongside individuals and families through seasons of learning, growth, and change. She also provides care and leadership for adults with mental health needs, creating spaces grounded in dignity, stability, and faith-informed compassion.

As a writer, Dawn speaks with honesty and tenderness, drawing from lived experience rather than theory. She believes that sometimes life's most meaningful work happens quietly, over time, and often without recognition. A Diamond from Clay reflects her conviction that what is formed in hidden places still carries purpose, value, and light.

As a new publisher, through Diamond Clay Publishing, Dawn seeks to create forthcoming projects as well as opportunities for others to be heard in a manner that inspires.

www.ingramcontent.com/pod-product-compliance
Lightning Source LLC
Chambersburg PA
CBHW030226170426
43194CB00007BA/871